JAN 2 9 2011

Anterooms

Works by Richard Wilbur

Responses: Prose Pieces, 1948–1976

Opposites

Molière's *The School for Wives* (translator)

Walking to Sleep: New Poems and Translations

Shakespeare: Poems (coeditor, with Alfred Harbage)

Molière's *Tartuffe* (translator)

The Poems of Richard Wilbur

Advice to a Prophet and Other Poems

Poe: Complete Poems (editor)

Candide: A Comic Operetta (with Lillian Hellman)

Poems, 1943–1956

Things of This World

A Bestiary (editor, with Alexander Calder)

Molière's *The Misanthrope* (translator)

Ceremony and Other Poems

The Beautiful Changes and Other Poems

Anterooms

New Poems and Translations

Richard Wilbur

HOUGHTON MIFFLIN HARCOURT

Boston   New York   2010

For information about permission to reproduce
selections from this book, write to Permissions,
Houghton Mifflin Harcourt Publishing Company,
215 Park Avenue South, New York, New York 10003.

www.hmhbooks.com

Library of Congress Cataloging-in-Publication Data
Wilbur, Richard, date.
Anterooms : new poems and translations / Richard Wilbur.
   p. cm.
ISBN 978-0-547-35811-6
I. Title.
PS3545.I32165A8 2010
811'.52 — dc22   2010005772

Book design by Melissa Lotfy
Printed in the United States of America

DOC 10 9 8 7 6 5 4 3 2 1

Some of these poems have appeared in *The New Yorker, Poetry,* the *Atlantic,* the *Yale Review, First Things,* the *Hopkins Review,* the *Raintown Review,* the *Alabama Literary Review,* and the *Riverbank Review.* In translating the riddles of Symphosius, I have been indebted (as always) to the scholarship of Raymond Theodore Ohl, and my poem "Trismegistus" is similarly indebted to Frances Yates. Daniel Hoffman's translation of Mallarmé's "Tombeau d'Edgar Poe" was published before mine, and I suspect that I owe him thanks for a crucial rhyme in the sestet. The unpublished fragment of Verlaine, included here, has been on deposit in the Houghton Library at Harvard; Stephen Sandy invited me to translate it for publication by the White Creek Press.

Contents

III

IV

The House

Sometimes, on waking, she would close her eyes
For a last look at that white house she knew
In sleep alone, and held no title to,
And had not entered yet, for all her sighs.

What did she tell me of that house of hers?
White gatepost; terrace; fanlight of the door;
A widow's walk above the bouldered shore;
Salt winds that ruffle the surrounding firs.

Is she now there, wherever there may be?
Only a foolish man would hope to find
That haven fashioned by her dreaming mind.
Night after night, my love, I put to sea.

I

A Measuring Worm

This yellow-striped green
Caterpillar, climbing up
The steep window screen,

Constantly (for lack
Of a full set of legs) keeps
Humping up his back.

It's as if he sent
By a sort of semaphore
Dark omegas meant

To warn of Last Things.
Although he doesn't know it,
He will soon have wings,

And I too don't know
Toward what undreamt condition
Inch by inch I go.

Flying

Treetops are not so high
Nor I so low
That I don't instinctively know
How it would be to fly

Through gaps that the wind makes, when
The leaves arouse
And there is a lifting of boughs
That settle and lift again.

Whatever my kind may be,
It is not absurd
To confuse myself with a bird
For the space of a reverie:

My species never flew,
But I somehow know
It is something that long ago
I almost adapted to.

Psalm

Give thanks for all things
On the plucked lute, and likewise
The harp of ten strings.

Have the lifted horn
Greatly blare, and pronounce it
Good to have been born.

Lend the breath of life
To the stops of the sweet flute
Or capering fife,

And tell the deep drum
To make, at the right juncture,
Pandemonium.

Then, in grave relief,
Praise too our sorrows on the
Cello of shared grief.

Young Orchard

These trees came to stay.
Planted at intervals of
Thirty feet each way,

Each one stands alone
Where it is to live and die.
Still, when they have grown

To full size, these trees
Will blend their crowns, and hum with
Mediating bees.

Meanwhile, see how they
Rise against their rootedness
On a gusty day,

Nodding one and all
To one another, as they
Rise again and fall,

Swept by flutterings
So that they appear a great
Consort of sweet strings.

Anterooms

Out of the snowdrift
Which covered it, this pillared
Sundial starts to lift,

Able now at last
To let its frozen hours
Melt into the past

In bright, ticking drops.
Time so often hastens by,
Time so often stops —

Still, it strains belief
How an instant can dilate,
Or long years be brief.

Dreams, which interweave
All our times and tenses, are
What we can believe:

Dark they are, yet plain,
Coming to us now as if
Through a cobwebbed pane

Where, before our eyes,
All the living and the dead
Meet without surprise.

Trismegistus

O Egypt, Egypt — so the great lament
Of thrice-great Hermes went —
Nothing of thy religion shall remain
Save fables, which thy children shall disdain.
His grieving eye foresaw
The world's bright fabric overthrown
Which married star to stone
And charged all things with awe.

And what, in that dismantled world, could be
More fabulous than he?
Had he existed? Was he but a name
Tacked on to forgeries which pressed the claim
Of every ancient quack —
That one could from a smoky cell
By talisman or spell
Coerce the Zodiac?

Still, still we summon him *at midnight hour*
To Milton's pensive tower,
And hear him tell again how, then and now,
Creation is a house of mirrors, how
Each herb that sips the dew
Dazzles the eye with many small
Reflections of the All —
Which, after all, is true.

Terza Rima

In this great form, as Dante proved in Hell,
There is no dreadful thing that can't be said
In passing. Here, for instance, one could tell

How our jeep skidded sideways toward the dead
Enemy soldier with the staring eyes,
Bumping a little as it struck his head,

And then flew on, as if toward Paradise.

Galveston, 1961

You who in crazy-lensed
Clear water fled your shape,
By choppy shallows flensed
And shaken like a cape,

Who gently butted down
Through weeds, and were unmade,
Piecemeal stirring your brown
Legs into stirred shade,

And rose, and with pastel
Coronas of your skin
Stained swell on glassy swell,
Letting them bear you in:

Now you have come to shore,
One woman and no other,
Sleek Panope no more,
Nor the vague sea our mother.

Shake out your spattering hair
And sprawl beside me here,
Sharing what we can share
Now that we are so near,

Small-talk and speechless love —
Mine being all but dumb
That knows so little of
What goddess you become

And still half-seem to be,
Though close and clear you lie,
Whom droplets of the sea
Emboss and magnify.

A Pasture Poem

This upstart thistle
Is young and touchy; it is
All barb and bristle,

Threatening to wield
Its green, jagged armament
Against the whole field.

Butterflies will dare
Nonetheless to lay their eggs
In that angle where

The leaf meets the stem,
So that ants or browsing cows
Cannot trouble them.

Summer will grow old
As will the thistle, letting
A clenched bloom unfold

To which the small hum
Of bee-wings and the flash of
Goldfinch-wings will come,

Till its purple crown
Blanches, and the breezes strew
The whole field with down.

Ecclesiastes 11:1

We must *cast our bread*
Upon the waters, as the
Ancient preacher said,

Trusting that it may
Amply be restored to us
After many a day.

That old metaphor,
Drawn from rice-farming on the
River's flooded shore,

Helps us to believe
That it's no great sin to give,
Hoping to receive.

Therefore I shall throw
Broken bread, this sullen day,
Out across the snow,

Betting crust and crumb
That birds will gather, and that
One more spring will come.

Soon

The sun in Aries
Shines on this plum tree full of risen sap,
And prints on last year's grass the map
Of a black river and its tributaries.

As yet no bud
Has broken, but we have not long to wait
For shadow-streams to merge in spate
And under blossoms deepen to a flood.

II

STÉPHANE MALLARMÉ:
The Tomb of Edgar Poe

Changed by eternity to Himself at last,
The Poet, with the bare blade of his mind,
Thrusts at a century which had not divined
Death's victory in his voice, and is aghast.

Aroused like some vile hydra of the past
When an angel proffered pure words to mankind,
Men swore that drunken squalor lay behind
His magic potions and the spells he cast.

The wars of earth and heaven — O endless grief!
If we cannot sculpt from them a bas-relief
To ornament the dazzling tomb of Poe,

Calm block here fallen from some far disaster,
Then let this boundary stone at least say no
To the dark flights of Blasphemy hereafter.

from the French

An Unpublished Poem

L'église tinte un angélus.
Le monde chante sa romance
Où vont et viennent quelques uns.
Mais l'autre elle est la règle immense.

Il n'est plus utile à l'esprit
De se préoccuper du coeur,
Ni pour l'âme qu'un coeur épuit
De s'en mettre plus en langueur.

Il est meilleur encore à l'âme
Que le coeur se souvient encore
Mais beaucoup moins que de la femme
Et beaucoup plus de tout encore.

The church-bell sounds the call to prayers.
Mankind intones its lovesick lay,
And in the city's thoroughfares
The latter music wins the day.

What use now for the mind to fret
Further about the heart's distress,
Or for the wearied soul to let
The heart protract its weariness?

Far better for the soul it were
If the heart retrieved its memory,
Recalling now far less of her
And more of all that is not she.

Horace II, 10

Neither should one, Licinius, beat forever
For the open sea, nor from a fear of gales
Become too cautious, and too closely hug
      The jagged shore.

A man who cherishes the golden mean
Has too much sense to live in a squalid house,
Yet sensibly eschews the sort of mansion
      That asks for envy.

It is the tall pine that the wind more cruelly
Buffets, the high tower that falls with the heavier
Crash; and it is the very crest of the mountain
      Where lightning strikes.

A heart that's well prepared for shifts of fortune
Hopes in adversity, and in happy times
Is wary. Jupiter brings afflicting winter,
      And the same god

Takes it away. Today's ill-luck will someday
Change for the better: sometimes Apollo wakens
The slumbering lyre to song, nor is he always
      Bending the bow.

In every hardship show yourself to be
Both brave and bold; yet when you run before
Too strong a favoring breeze, wisely take in
      Your swelling sails.

from the Latin

Two Nativity Poems

Presepio

The wise men; Joseph; the tiny infant; Mary;
The cows; the drovers, each with his dromedary;
The hulking shepherds in their sheepskins — they
Have all become toy figures made of clay.

In the cotton-batting snow that's strewn with glints,
A fire is blazing. You'd like to touch that tinsel
Star with a finger — or all five of them,
As the infant wished to do in Bethlehem.

All this, in Bethlehem, was of greater size.
Yet the clay, round which the drifted cotton lies,
With tinsel overhead, feels good to be
Enacting what we can no longer see.

Now you are huge compared to them, and high
Beyond their ken. Like a midnight passerby
Who finds the pane of some small hut aglow,
You peer from the cosmos at this little show.

There life goes on, although the centuries
Require that some diminish by degrees,
While others grow, like you. The small folk there
Contend with granular snow and icy air,

And the smallest reaches for the breast, and you
Half-wish to clench your eyes, or step into
A different galaxy, in whose wastes there shine
More lights than there are sands in Palestine.

25. XII. 1993

To M. V.

For a miracle, take one shepherd's sheepskin, throw
In a pinch of now, a grain of long ago,
And a handful of tomorrow. Add by eye
A little chunk of space, a piece of sky,

And it will happen. For miracles, gravitating
To earth, know just where people will be waiting,
And eagerly will find the right address
And tenant, even in a wilderness.

Or, if you're leaving home, switch on a new
Four-pointed star, then, as you say adieu,
To light a vacant world with steady blaze
And follow you forever with its gaze.

from the Russian

III

Out Here

Strangers might wonder why
That big snow-shovel's leaning
Against the house in July.
Has it some cryptic meaning?

It means at least to say
That, here, we needn't be neat
About putting things away,
As on some suburban street.

What's more, by leaning there
The shovel seems to express,
With its rough and ready air,
A boast of ruggedness.

If a stranger said in sport
"I see you're prepared for snow,"
Our shovel might retort
"Out here, you never know."

The Censor

In any company, he listens hard
For signs of vanity and self-regard,
Reacting to each name that's dropped, to each
Complacent anecdote or turn of speech
With subtle indications of surprise —
A wince, perhaps, a widening of the eyes,
Or a slight lifting of the brow, addressed
To the egomaniac within his breast.

A Reckoning

At my age, one begins
To chalk up all his sins,
Hoping to wipe the slate
Before it is too late.

Therefore I call to mind
All memories of the kind
That make me writhe and sweat
And tremble with regret.

What do these prove to be?
In every one I see
Shocked faces that, alas,
Now know me for an ass.

Fatuities that I
Have uttered, drunk or dry,
Return now in a rush
And make my old cheek blush.

But how can I repent
From mere embarrassment?
Damn-foolishness can't well
Entitle me to Hell.

Well, I shall put the blame
On the pride that's in my shame.
Of that, I must be shriven
If I'm to be forgiven.

A Prelude

Matthew Arnold, looking over
The Channel from the cliffs of Dover,
Scanned with his telescope almost
The whole French coast
As far as Étretat,
And was upon the point of saying "Ah,"
When he perceived, not far from the great Aiguille,
A lobster led on a leash beside the sea.
It was Nerval, enjoying his *vacances!*
Alas for gravitas! *Hélas* for *France!*
Having of late been panicky
About culture and anarchy,
Arnold now left in a hurry,
Foreseeing a night of worry.

The President's Song to the Baron

Intended for a musical version of Jean Giraudoux's *La Folle de Chaillot*

THE PRESIDENT

Ah, Baron . . .
Think how the world would run,
Think how the wheels would spin
Think how we'd get things done,
Think how we'd rake it in,
If these vivid personalities who make our life a hell
Were knocked down and reassembled as efficient *Personnel* . . .

I dream of a column of miners approaching a mine
With mechanical step and with profiles of standard design,
And a single desire in the depths of their corporate soul:
To surprise you and me by exceeding their quota of coal.
Ah, me!

THE BARON

Ah, me!

THE PRESIDENT

What a workable world this could be,
If the laboring creature were programmed
        to slave like a drone
With a head full of circuits and no damned
        ideas of his own!
How we'd cherish the dear fellow then! How he'd
        capture our hearts!
A standardized laboring man with replaceable parts!

I dream of the desert, I dream of a long caravàn
That consists of an infinite line of the very same man,
And their camels are bringing us riches in baskets and sacks,
With a uniform number of humps on their dutiful backs.
Ah, me!

THE BARON

Ah, me!

THE PRESIDENT

What a livable world this will be
When the millwork and fieldwork and dockwork
                  are done to our liking
By creatures who function like clockwork
                  but don't dream of striking!
What a luscious conception, far sweeter than babas or tarts!
A standardized laboring man with replaceable parts!

Some Words Inside of Words

(for children and others)

A cat will often take the softest chair
In the living room, and lie for hours there
With a smug, sleepy look upon his face,
Behaving just as if he owned the place.
Therefore it's no surprise to notice how
Inside *homeowner* is the word *meow.*

*

The barnacle is found in salty seas,
Clinging to rocks in crusty colonies;
And salt, which chemists call *NaCl,*
Is found inside the *barnacle* as well.

*

What could be sillier than for a *cow*
To try to cross the ocean in a *scow?*
With such a captain, to my way of thinking,
The wretched vessel would be sure of sinking!
No one should be entrusted with a rudder
Who has two horns and four hooves and an udder.

*

If a *carp* is in your *carport,* go find out
Whether the living room is full of trout
And eels and salamanders, and if there's
A snapping turtle paddling up the stairs.
If that's what's going on, your house (beyond
A doubt) is at the bottom of a pond.

*

At heart, *ambassadors* are always *sad.*
Why? Because world affairs are always bad,
So that they're always having to express
"Regret," and "grave concern," and "deep distress."

*

Some snakes are nice to handle, but an *asp*
Is not the kind to take within your *grasp.*
That is what Cleopatra did, I fear,
And, as you know, she is no longer here.

*

The *roc*'s a huge, bold, hungry bird who's able
To eat an elephant (so says the fable).
No farmer likes to see one feasting cockily
Right in the middle of his field of *broccoli.*

*

In every *ice cube* there's a *cub,* and so
It sometimes happens that a cub will grow
Inside the freezer of a Frigidaire,
Until it is a full-sized polar bear.
What happens then? Well, opening the door,
It steps into the kitchen with a roar
And lumbers through the house, fierce, white, and fat,
Turning down every single thermostat.

IV

Thirty-seven Riddles from Symphosius

1. Nebula

I wear night's face, although not black of skin,
And at high noon I bring the darkness in,
Ere Cynthia's beams, or starlight, can begin.

2. Glacies

I once was water, and soon shall be again.
Strict heaven binds me now by many a chain.
I crack when trodden, and when held give pain.

3. Nix

Light dust of water fallen from the sky,
I'm wet in summer and in winter dry.
Ere I make rivers, whole lands I occupy.

4. Navis

Long daughter of the forest, swift of pace,
In whom old neighbors join as beam and brace,
I speed on many paths, yet leave no trace.

5. Aranea

Athena schooled me in the weaver's trade.
The robes I make require no shuttle's aid.
I have no hands; by feet my works are made.

6. *Rana*

Down at the pond, a raucous voice I raise
In praiseful song, but it's myself I praise.
I'm ever singing, but no one lauds my lays.

7. *Mus*

My house is small, but I never lock the door.
Simply I live, upon a stolen store.
My Latin name a Roman consul bore.

8. *Formica*

I'm provident, and I'm not an idle bum.
I lug home food before the snowflakes come.
Not in great loads, of course, but crumb by crumb.

9. *Musca*

A pest, on every noisome thing I prey.
I shun the cold, but love a summer's day,
Though man-made breezes frighten me away.

10. *Cornix*

Nine lives I have, if Greece may be believed.
I always dress in black, though not bereaved.
Angry or not, I sound extremely peeved.

11. Vespertilio

My Latin name is from the start of night.
I have no feathers, though I've wings for flight.
I come with darkness and I flee the light.

12. Pediculus

Here's a new game of catch that all can play:
If you catch it, you needn't keep it; or you may,
If you don't catch it, keep it anyway.

13. Malva

My feet are like a goose's, I confess,
And more than two of them do I possess,
Yet all those feet are upside-down, no less.

14. Molae

Two stones are we who close together lie.
The first is lazy and the second spry.
One's moved to move; the other doesn't try.

15. Pila

I have no tresses, whether dark or fair.
Inside, where none can see it, is my hair.
Hands send me and return me through the air.

16. *Ancora*

One piece of iron joins my two flukes together.
I strive against the waves, and windy weather.
Searching the deep, in earth I fix my tether.

17. *Malleus*

My bodily strength's not matchless everywhere,
But head for head I am beyond compare;
Large is my head, and all my weight is there.

18. *Clavis*

Great powers I have, small though my strength may be.
Doors close and open through my potency.
The master's house I guard, and he guards me.

19. *Ericius*

In a prickly house lives one whose life is charmed.
Within an armory he dwells unarmed.
His back is pierced with spears, yet he's unharmed.

20. *Funambulus*

Through middle air, where earth and heaven meet,
A walker goes, with steps adept and neat,
Upon a path more narrow than his feet.

21. *Tigris*

I'm named for a river, or it's named for me.
Yoked to the wind, I'm swifter far than he.
I need no mate; wind sires my progeny.

22. *Rosa*

Earth's crimson blush am I; it's beauty's hue.
I'm ringed by spears that run intruders through.
If only I lived longer than I do!

23. *Viola*

Great virtues, though I'm small, to me belong;
I'm delicate, but my perfume is strong;
Thornless, I need not blush for any wrong.

24. *Tus*

Sweet scent of Araby which flames consume,
To please the gods I burn in fire and fume,
Though not deserving of a sinner's doom.

25. *Pistillus*

All things I powerfully crush and blend.
I have one neck, with a head at either end.
To more anatomy I don't pretend.

26. *Vinum in Acetum Conversum*

Nothing's been either added to me or
Withdrawn, yet what I was I am no more.
I start to be what I was not before.

27. *Anulus cum Gemma*

I cling to an extremity. You might say
I'm part of it, so little do I weigh.
My face makes good impressions every day.

28. *Papaver*

My head is large, but what's within are small.
I've one leg only, but it's very tall.
Sleep loves me, but I get no sleep at all.

29. *Talpa*

Blind is my face, which darkness hides from you.
The day is night to me, no sun I view,
And I, beneath the sod, am hidden too.

30. *Harundo*

A god's sweet mistress, by a river nursed;
The Muses' caroler; in black immersed,
I tell by hand what head has pondered first.

31. Cochlea

Upon my back a house and home I bear,
Prepared to move where heaven bids me fare,
And so am not an exile anywhere.

32. Luscus Alium Vendens

Though you may think I'm talking tommyrot,
One eye and a thousand heads is what he's got.
Can he sell what he has, and buy what he has not?

33. Miles Podagricus

A fierce and fearless warrior was I.
Six feet I stood, as no one dared deny,
But now I've barely two, from living high.

34. Pluvia

Hurled out of heaven on a downward track,
I fall to earth through gloom and thunder-crack,
Yet here I'm taken in and welcomed back.

35. Umbra

From sneaky foes I need not fear the worst.
By this one gift my worries are dispersed—
That none can budge me who does not budge first.

36. Clepsydra

Good governor of speech, firm judge of quiet,
Just chastener of those whose tongues run riot,
I flow while verbiage flows, till wearied by it.

37. Echo

I'm a shy maiden, properly repressed;
I don't speak out; that wouldn't be *modeste;*
But I am glad to answer when addressed.

from the Latin

Symphosius (fourth century A.D.?) was the author of one hundred Latin riddles. The answers to those in the preceding selection are as follows:

1. Cloud
2. Ice
3. Snow
4. Ship
5. Spider
6. Frog
7. Mouse
8. Ant
9. Fly
10. Crow
11. Bat
12. Louse
13. Mallow
14. Millstones
15. Ball
16. Anchor
17. Hammer
18. Key
19. Hedgehog
20. Tightrope walker
21. Tigress
22. Rose
23. Violet
24. Incense
25. Pestle
26. Wine turned to vinegar
27. Seal ring
28. Poppy
29. Mole
30. Reed
31. Snail
32. One-eyed garlic vendor
33. Gouty soldier
34. Rain
35. Shadow
36. Water clock
37. Echo